The Days of Creation by Heart

THE BIBLE BY HEART Series

The DAYS OF CREATION by Heart

Teaching Children How God Made the World

Written by Dr. James Moseley and Dr. Gina Loudon
Illustrated by Mike Sofka

BEYOND WORDS
Portland, Oregon

1750 S.W. Skyline Blvd., Suite 20
Portland, Oregon 97221-2543
503–531–8700/503–531–8773 fax
www.beyondword.com

This first Beyond Words hardcover edition August 2025

Copyright © 2025 by Summerwind Media Works

All rights reserved, including the right to reproduce this book or portions thereof in any form whatsoever without the prior written permission of Beyond Words Publishing, Inc., except where permitted by law.

Editor: Michele Ashtiani Cohn
Design: Mike Sofka

The text of this book was set in Adobe Caslon Pro and Jack Armstrong Regular.
The illustrations for this book were rendered in Adobe Photoshop.

Beyond Words Publishing is an imprint of Simon & Schuster, LLC,
and the Beyond Words logo is a registered trademark of Beyond Words Publishing, Inc.

For more information about special discounts for bulk purchases,
please contact Beyond Words Special Sales at 503–531–8700 or specialsales@beyondword.com.

Manufactured in the United States of America

10 9 8 7 6 5 4 3 2 1

ISBN 978-1-58270-969-7 (hardcover)
ISBN 978-1-58270-971-0 (ebook)

The corporate mission of Beyond Words Publishing, Inc.: *Inspire to Integrity*

Dedication
To all our beloved children.

The Days of Creation by Heart

Day 1
Time begins and with it light.

Day 2
The sky unfurls so vast and bright.

Day 3
Sea and land and flowers and pine.

Day 4
Sun and moon and stars that shine.

Day 5
Fish that swim and birds that call.

Day 6
Beasts and Adam over all.

Day 7
All is blessed by God at rest.

DAY 2
THE SKY UNFURLS
SO VAST AND BRIGHT.

GENESIS 1:6-8

NOW, CHILDREN, ON THE FOLLOWING PAGES, USE YOUR IMAGINATION TO DRAW WHAT YOU THINK WAS SPECIAL ABOUT EACH OF THE DAYS!

DAY 1: TIME BEGINS AND WITH IT LIGHT.

GENESIS 1:1-5

DAY 2: THE SKY UNFURLS SO VAST AND BRIGHT.

GENESIS 1:6-8

DAY 3: SEA AND LAND AND FLOWERS AND PINE.

GENESIS 1:9-13

DAY 4: SUN AND MOON AND STARS THAT SHINE.

GENESIS 1:14-19

DAY 5: FISH THAT SWIM AND BIRDS THAT CALL.

GENESIS 1:20-23

DAY 6: BEASTS AND ADAM OVER ALL.

GENESIS 1:24-31

DAY 7: ALL IS BLESSED BY GOD AT REST.

GENESIS 2:1-3

From Dr. Gina Loudon . . .

Why We Wrote This Book

*"Train up a child in the way he should go, and when he is old,
he will not depart from it."* (Proverbs 22:6)

Memorizing Scripture is more than just learning words—it's shaping a child's heart and mind with God's truth. The verses we learn as children stay with us for life, offering wisdom, comfort, and guidance when we need it most.

When Jim and I created this book, we wanted to help children absorb not just Scripture but also the order of God's creation, making it easy to recall and understand. Research shows that what we learn early stays with us, and memory techniques like repetition and visualization make learning even stronger. So where better to begin than "In the beginning…"?

How To Use This Book

"Thy word have I hid in mine heart, that I might not sin against Thee." (Psalm 119:11)

The best way to use this book is through repetition—read it at bedtime or any time your child is ready to listen. Encourage them to draw their own pictures of what they've learned, making the story personal and memorable.

For the best reinforcement, have them teach the story back to you. Nothing deepens understanding like sharing it with someone else!

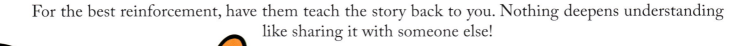

From Dr. James Moseley . . .

A Little Biblical Encouragement for Parents

When you read to your children, "In the beginning, God created the heavens and the earth" (Genesis 1:1), you are not sharing a fairy tale—you are sharing Truth.

God existed before time began. He created everything in six days—whether those were 24-hour days or long epochs is open to debate, but either way, Genesis remains true. Science and Scripture are not at odds. As Galileo wisely said, "The Bible tells us how to go to heaven, not how the heavens go."

Evolution is still a theory, not a proven law. Many scientists now recognize flaws in Darwinian evolution, yet it remains widely accepted—not because of strong evidence, but because challenging it is unpopular. If you're interested in more information, check out my website, thebiblehistoryguy.com.

You don't need to be a scientist to teach your children the truth. By reading Genesis, you are giving them knowledge that has stood the test of time—truth that was valid thousands of years ago and will remain so for generations to come.

About the Authors

Dr. James Moseley holds a PhD in Bible Exposition from Liberty University, where he also serves as Director of International Partnerships. The author of more than two dozen books on theology, history, and fiction, he is widely recognized as "The Bible History Guy" on *American Sunrise* on Real America's Voice. A seasoned traveler who has lived and worked in 77 countries, he also writes screenplays and short stories and is fluent in Italian with working knowledge of four other languages. His acclaimed children's series, beginning with *The Days of Creation by Heart*, brings biblical truth to life in unforgettable ways for young readers. He and his wife, Madlene, share a love for culinary arts, golden retrievers, and making memories with their children and grandchildren.

Dr. Gina Loudon (aka "Dr. Gina") is a Christian media personality, author, and political commentator. She holds a PhD in psychology and human development and has hosted radio and TV shows, including *Dr. Gina Prime Time* and *American Sunrise* on Real America's Voice. She served as a media surrogate for Donald Trump's 2016 campaign, cochaired Women for Trump in 2020, and has appeared on major networks like Fox News and CNN. She's a bestselling author and contributes to outlets like FoxNews.com and Breitbart. Dr. Loudon and her husband, former Missouri State Senator John Loudon, have five children. She also founded They All Have Names, a nonprofit to support special needs adoption.

About the Illustrator

Mike Sofka is an illustrator and designer who contributed to several *VeggieTales* productions, including *The League of Incredible Vegetables* (2012) and *The Penniless Princess* (2012). His work encompassed both visual design and voice acting roles. Beyond VeggieTales, Sofka has collaborated with organizations such as the Walt Disney Company. He currently operates his own illustration and design business.